wedding FLOWERS

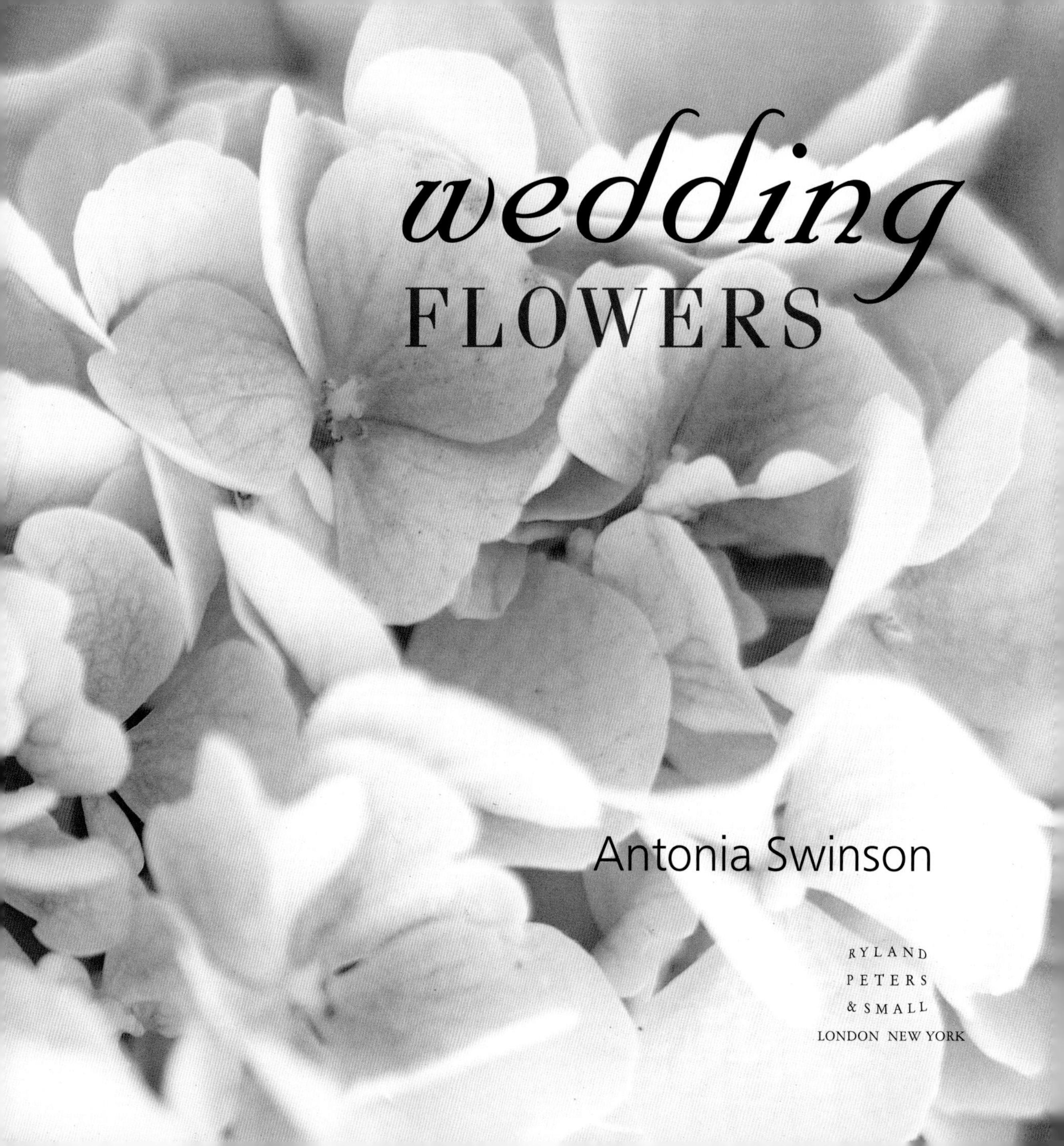

wedding
FLOWERS

Antonia Swinson

RYLAND
PETERS
& SMALL
LONDON NEW YORK

Senior Designer	Liz Sephton
Senior Editor	Clare Double
Picture Research	Emily Westlake
Production	Gemma Moules
Publishing Director	Alison Starling

First published in the US in 2008 by
Ryland Peters & Small
519 Broadway, 5th Floor
New York, NY 10012
www.rylandpeters.com

10 9 8 7 6 5 4

Text, design, and photographs
© Ryland Peters & Small 2008

Library of Congress Cataloging-in-
Publication Data
Swinson, Antonia.
  Wedding flowers / Antonia Swinson.
    p. cm.
  Includes index.
  ISBN 978-1-84597-456-5
1. Wedding decorations. 2. Flower
arrangement. 3. Bridal bouquets. I.
Title.
  SB449.5.W4S95 2008
  745.92'6--dc22
                          2007022108

Printed and bound in China.

contents

Introduction

Every wedding is a reflection of the personalities and tastes of the bride and groom. Flowers play a big part in setting the scene for the day and, depending on which varieties are chosen, their colors, and the designs they are part of, can help to conjure up any number of different styles and moods. Nowadays there isn't a supermarket in the land in which you can't buy a huge range of flowers sourced from all over the world. This breadth of choice opens up all kinds of possibilities, but it can be hard to know where to start, particularly if you are unfamiliar with flowers and how they're arranged.

This book is designed to inspire and inform, to act as a comprehensive style resource for anyone embarking

on the process of choosing their wedding flowers. There are sections covering all the sorts of arrangements you might want on the day: bridal bouquets; flowers for the bridesmaids; floral headdresses and accessories; boutonnieres and corsages; and flowers for the reception, including table centerpieces, place settings, and favors. Each section covers lots of different styles of arrangement and uses of color. There are color schemes that are pale, vibrant, cool and hot; and styles such as traditional, modern, romantic, minimalist, formal, and rustic.

The first decision to be taken about flowers is usually what the bride will carry, and from this key starting point ideas can develop for all the other floral

arrangements needed on the day. Sometimes a bride
will have particular flowers in mind for her bouquet,
such as roses or lilies. Sometimes color will be the key:
the bride might want all her wedding flowers to be
white or cream, for instance.

The style to which the bride and groom are
aspiring is crucial: for example, if the wedding is to be
modern and minimalist, certain flowers will reflect this
better than others (calla lilies and orchids have the right
sort of structural quality; carnations don't). Or, if the
wedding is a laid-back family occasion at a small church,
with the reception in a tent, cottage-garden flowers such
as sweet peas, pinks, and stocks will be a charming

complement. The seasons can play an influential role, too. For a wedding taking place just before Christmas, for instance, what could be more natural than to be inspired by the colors of the season: the dark green of evergreen foliage, the red of holly berries, and the white of snow and frost? In spring, the presence of lots of white, yellow, and blue flowers in the landscape might inspire a palette of narcissi, spring snowdrops, and forget-me-nots.

Choosing your wedding flowers should be a happy and exciting process, and whether your taste runs to a big bouquet of electric-blue dyed roses or a little posy of lily of the valley picked from the garden, flowers will help to make your day the glorious celebration you've dreamed of.

Flowers for the Bride

Introduction

The bride is undeniably the star of any wedding, so her flowers are also the focus of much attention. The wedding dress is the key stylistic element of the day, so its design, fabric, and color will shape ideas for the bouquet. A traditional white or off-white dress is a flattering backdrop to flowers of any color, from whites and pastels to brights. If the dress is a different color, whether palest pink or rich gold, the flowers need to be chosen with more care to avoid an unflattering clash.

White is still the classic choice for the bouquet as much as the dress; pastels are romantic and easy to work with; deeper colors, such as rich purples or sultry reds, are trickier to use but can look spectacular. Certain colors seem to lend themselves to the quality of the light in each

season: blue-reds and greens in winter; blue, white, and yellow in spring; clear bright pinks, blues, and purples in the strong summer light; and warm, mellow yellows and oranges in the fall. Think about the shape of the bouquet, too. The most traditional is a teardrop or "shower" shape, using wired flowers, though simpler tied bouquets are now very popular. You could also opt for a generous bouquet designed to be carried over the arm.

Whether you choose a large loose bouquet or a neat domed one depends partly on the shape of your dress; don't let the flowers dominate the ensemble. For instance, a sheaf of calla lilies would perfectly complement a slim A-line dress, while a full-skirted gown could carry off a large, dramatic bouquet.

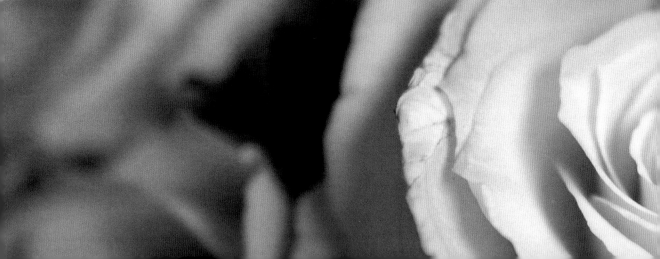

TRADITIONAL
BOUQUETS
cool and pastel colors

The stems of this bouquet are bound in striped ribbon, secured with pearl-headed pins.
The color scheme is white with tiny touches of *blue and pink*, achieved with roses,
stocks, veronicas, larkspurs, and *bachelor's buttons*.

This large, loose bouquet, tied with wide white ribbon, has a *cottage-garden feel*. The round, soft *peonies* complement the roses well, with *delicate dill flowers* and bridal wreath flowers and foliage adding further interest.

This white bouquet is *timelessly elegant*. With its fanned shape, it's designed to be carried gracefully *over the arm*, showing off to the full its combination of roses, loosestrife, lilac, and *eucalyptus*, all tied with sheer white ribbon.

Grand but not overly formal, this *dramatic* hand-tied shower bouquet for a *winter wedding* contrasts pure white flowers with dark, glossy foliage. Exquisite *camellias* and early-flowering clematis partner their own foliage and cascading lengths of ivy.

This tied bouquet, finished with *sheer pink ribbon*, has a nicely compact but full look that shows off the *soft roundness* of the flower heads beautifully. It uses lavender and ruscus foliage, hyacinths, bouvardia, alliums, and *snapdragons*.

This bouquet is bigger, looser, and more dramatic. It's composed of *huge pink lilies* and roses, *photinia foliage* and flowers, kangaroo paw, and *pink-budded jasmine*, all tied with a large bow of bronze-green ribbon.

21

Although painstakingly made, this wired, teardrop bouquet has a lovely *sense of movement*.
The emphasis is on color, with *pale and deep pink roses*, lilac and purple Singapore orchids,
veronicas, ruscus foliage, and *asparagus fern*.

This dense mass of blooms—three varieties of rose, stock, and *freesia*—tied with **old-gold ribbon**, is a romantic combination of white, cream, and soft pink, with wired **rhinestone beads** adding sparkle.

This sheaf of calla or arum lilies is spectacular in its *sculptural simplicity*. The long stems
have been tied with very wide *pewter ribbon*, producing an arrangement that would be
the ideal match for an *A-line dress*.

These *scented longiflorum lilies* have been given a more relaxed treatment by making a few stems into a loose bunch with white *loosestrife*, whose graceful *arching heads* complement the lilies' tapering petals.

This little bouquet of pink-and-white *ranunculus* couldn't be simpler or *prettier*.
The stems have been bound with layered satin ribbon, *lace*, and velvet ribbon,
fastened with a bead on a pin.

Green and pink is always a pleasing combination, and this full bouquet partners
pinkish-mauve roses and green-and-pink *hydrangeas*, with the unusual
accompaniment of *poppy seed heads* and marjoram.

Soft pink, lilac, and green create a *restful scheme* in this summer bouquet. There are blowsy peonies and roses, *blue flag irises*, clematis, and hebe and skimmia foliage, tied with ribbons in purple and *cerise*.

The long tails of ribbon tying this bouquet are reminiscent of maypoles and contribute to its *informal, rustic look*. Roses, lupines, *delphiniums*, stocks, and daisies, in white, pink, yellow, and blue look *fresh and summery*.

True blues are rare in the flower world, but this large, cascading bouquet uses some of the best examples. Stately delphiniums, *sea holly*, and ivy erupt from a base of sky-blue *mophead hydrangeas*.

In the garden, lilac is a ***herald of early summer***. For this large bouquet, two varieties have
been casually bunched together, their long stems bound with wide, ***deep purple ribbon***
and white lace, then finished with a flamboyant bow.

31

Bridal bouquets have their origins in the *posies of herbs* once carried on the wedding day to ward off evil spirits. Traditional *ribbon streamers* decorate this modern version, composed of rosemary, *golden marjoram*, thyme, sage, and tarragon.

This bouquet is in the formal *Victorian style*, with the flowers wired into circles. However, a cool palette of green and blue in the form of galax leaves, *guelder rose*, hyacinths, and *lisianthus* gives it a modern slant.

TRADITIONAL
BOUQUETS
hot and intense colors

Sweet peas usually come in a *glorious array* of white, pink, purple, and red. These, however, are an exceptional mixture of *cream, yellow, apricot, and orange* and have been gathered into a huge bunch with *lady's mantle* for contrast.

Flowers for the Bride

In a variation, the same sweet peas have been interspersed with huge *scarlet anemones* to make a **bold** but not garish bouquet. Egg-yolk yellow ribbon and a *ruff of lemon-yellow* net add to the vivacious effect.

This intensely colored, *sophisticated bouquet* of roses, senecio, galax, and *silvery cones* has been designed for a *winter wedding*, when the thin light will heighten the drama of the blue-toned reds and cool greens.

Flowers for the Bride

Another winter bouquet, this time its deep reds and greens *lifted* by the inclusion of *white*.
Four varieties of rose have been joined by *skimmia buds* and leaves, laurustinus, and
black-berried ivy.

Red and pink is a *daring combination*, but the result here is stunning. A mixture of pink, red, and *black-red roses* has been used, along with sweet peas, scarlet *glory lilies*, and skimmia, finished with a funky checked ribbon.

This dressy bouquet of **white and purple ranunculus**, black-red roses, and pink and purple
sweet peas, its stems bound with **gleaming ribbon**, suggests a late-afternoon wedding and
evening reception, black tie, and dancing.

41

The poppy anemones, ranunculus, and sweet peas in this bouquet span the purple spectrum, from *lilac* to plum and *royal purple*, with sumptuous and dramatic results. ***Two ribbons***, one satin, one sheer, finish the arrangement.

The shape of this bouquet of glowing poppy anemones, lilac, and *hebe foliage* is very different from the one opposite. It is unstructured and *naturalistic*, suggesting, perhaps, a laid-back *country wedding* rather than a grand metropolitan one.

CONTEMPORARY BOUQUETS
cool and pastel colors

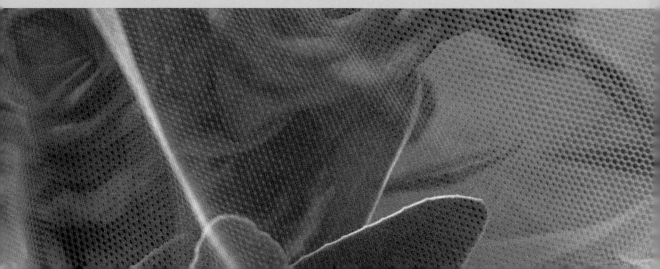

This bouquet of magnificent calla or arum lilies is ***cool and modern***. The stems' length is emphasized by the blades of ***bear grass***, some of which have clear beads threaded onto them. Sheer lilac ribbon and ***silver beaded wire*** (just seen) bind the stems.

Flowers for the Bride

This winter bouquet shows that even bare twigs can look glamorous and beautiful. *Willow stems* and skimmia leaves have been *misted with gold* spray paint and arranged with *white roses*, then tied with gold ribbon.

Simple and classic, this bouquet of white roses proves the old adage that *less is more*.
A bow of diaphanous ribbon is a good way of echoing an *accent color*—matching the
bridesmaids' dresses, for example.

Roses that have absorbed dyed water through their stems are available in some extraordinary colors. These *electric blue* ones will only appeal to a few, but *swathed in tulle* and partnered by senecio leaves, they look unmistakably *bridal*.

49

These ranunculus show how interesting pale can be. With their huge black, *feathery centers* and *pink-tinged white petals*, they're undeniably glamorous, particularly when finished with a collar of *silver organdy* and cranberry ribbon.

Eucharis lilies have an *exotic and fragile* beauty. Here, the bride, who wears an
understated silk A-line dress, holds a small, loose posy of them to complement
the *luxurious minimalism* of her ensemble.

This dense bouquet of lemon-yellow tulips is warm and cheerful, its stems bound in *cream wire-edged ribbon*. Tulips are *star flowers*, being good value, long lasting, and available all year in *myriad colors*.

Neat, light, and *easy to carry*, the stems of this bouquet of pompomlike *mimosa* and
miniature narcissi are bound by exquisite *floral braid*, a detail which is as much a thing
of beauty as the flowers themselves.

Contemporary Bouquets • Cool and Pastel Colors

With its slender *grass-green leaves* and lanternlike orange flowers, *sandersonia* is a
beautiful oddity. It's so distinctive that it deserves to be used alone, here gathered into
a huge, loose sheaf and tied with *bronze organdy ribbon*.

This **green on green** bouquet mixes exotic cymbidium orchids, **kangaroo paw**, and galax leaves with frothy lady's mantle, a **cottage-garden favorite**. It's unconventional, certainly, but shows what scope an all-green color scheme can offer.

CONTEMPORARY
BOUQUETS
hot and intense colors

Although tulips are spring flowering in the garden, they're available in florists all year. Here, in rich *orange and maroon*, they have an *autumnal* feel. Binding the stems in heavy wire gives the arrangement a *contemporary twist*.

Flowers for the Bride

This grand, even extravagant bouquet puts the focus on *intense color*, with roses, *Iceland poppies*, and ranunculus in shades of *burnt orange*, tangerine, *vermilion*, and golden yellow against a dark background of hebe, skimmia, and coral fern.

59

With their blue undertones, the two varieties of red rose used for this *glamorous* domed bouquet
look particularly good in *winter*. Here, they're framed by *folded aspidistra leaves*, buffed up
with a little oil for extra gleam.

This sophisticated bouquet in shades of red and burgundy has lots of *textural interest*: velvety roses, silky peonies, and chenillelike *cockscomb* and *love-lies-bleeding*. Plum-colored ribbon ties the stems.

61

Perfect for a **Christmas wedding**, this bouquet captures the essence of the season, with blood-red roses, **scarlet amaryllis**, winter jasmine, camellia leaves, **pine foliage**, variegated ivy, and silver cones, all tied with a huge forest-green bow.

Exuberant and *tropical*, this is a bouquet for the adventurous bride. Cool green
palm leaves frame heliconias and *ginger lilies*, looking like birds of paradise in
shades of coral, orange, and pinkish red.

The *rich colors of autumn* have been gathered together in this exquisite bouquet, which combines fruits, flowers, and foliage—oak leaves, roses, *cape gooseberries*, hypericum berries, *kumquats*, and skimmia flowers.

Flowers for the Bride

Tied with cream satin ribbon, this unusual little bunch of **pink-budded skimmia** and red-spotted orange **vanda orchids** shows that even the smallest and simplest of arrangements can make a strong statement.

Fun and unconventional, this bouquet is a **bold** but carefully **balanced** mixture of colors. There are lilac and purple sweet peas; **pink, orange, and purple** ranunculus; and white camellias, finished with multicolored ribbon and burgundy net.

This lush bouquet has a collar of *variegated hosta* leaves encircling scented blue hyacinths and silky-petaled purple *gloxinias*, a flower usually sold in garden centers as an indoor plant. *Shimmering* purple organdy ribbon ties the stems.

Black and white is a daringly dramatic combination. These deep purple *calla or arum lilies*
are about as close to black as flowers get and make a *sultry partner* for pure white ones,
their stems tied with blades of steel grass.

This ***black and white bouquet*** is somewhat softer and more romantic. Black-red roses balance
white ranunculus and poppy anemones, whose feathery centers are a true black. A ruff of
galax leaves and black-and-gold ribbon finishes the picture.

This spectacular modern arrangement of *painter's palettes*, snake grass, and *aspidistra leaves* is part bouquet, part *sculpture*, thanks to the soldering wire that has been looped around the stems and over the top of the flowers.

This bouquet of mauve, gold, orange, *pale apricot*, and deep red roses, framed by camellia leaves, shows how *gorgeous* unusual color combinations can be. Fine-gauge colored wire has been woven over the flowers like *spun sugar*.

FINISHING
TOUCHES

A *wrist corsage* could take the place of a conventional bridal bouquet. Here, pristine *eucharis lilies* have been used, with individual heads pinned to long lengths of *white satin* ribbon.

This single, *perfect rose* in a shade of palest pink is a simple but stunning alternative to a *tiara*, anchoring a waist-length tulle veil. Any *floral headdress* needs careful pinning to make sure it stays in place all day.

Roses are a *good choice* for headdresses because they'll stand up well to a day's celebrations and still look good at the end of the reception. These *ivory roses* have been interspersed with *variegated ivy* leaves.

Flowers for the Bride

The *intense reds* of this headdress look very striking against the bride's dark hair.
The *texture* of the flowers—a rose, ruffled cockscomb, and tassels of *love-lies-bleeding*
—is such that they look as though they could be made from fabric.

Finishing Touches

Sweet peas in every shade of purple from lilac to *plum* have
been wired onto a headband to make this headdress,
carefully graduated from pale to dark shades.

This bride has chosen *seasonal flowers* for her winter wedding. A single
flawless camellia and early-flowering clematis flowers and foliage have been
wired into a headdress that anchors a *full-length veil*.

In place of a headdress, *single flowerets* of green hydrangea and *soft pink roses*
have been pinned into this bride's tumbling, Pre-Raphaelite curls to give
a relaxed, natural look.

Flowers for the Bride

Far more *memorable* than a "just married" sign, a large wreath of white *daisies*,
finished with a ribbon bow, decorates the trunk of the newlyweds' car, ready for
them to make a *stylish getaway*.

Flowers for the Bridesmaids

Introduction

The bridesmaids' flowers must complement the bride's
but not outshine them, and it's appropriate for them to
be discernibly different. They should follow the same
broad color and floral scheme, at the same time offering
an interesting variation on it. For instance, if the bridal
bouquet consists of white roses bound with pink satin
ribbon, the bridesmaids might carry posies of pink spray
roses tied with white ribbon.

Bridesmaids can carry bouquets or posies (it's usual
for their arrangements to be smaller than the bride's),
which can be complemented by hair accessories such as
floral barettes or combs. A wrist corsage makes a stylish

alternative to a traditional posy; another option is a chic bag filled with flowers (which can be taken home to keep afterward). Flowergirls can be given bags or small wicker baskets to carry. They're a good practical choice: accessories and arrangements for children must be comfortable and easy to hold, ideally given to their recipients at the very last minute to avoid damage to fragile blooms. Old-fashioned charm is usually a very successful look for little girls: May Queen-style circlets; floral headbands; posies with ribbon streamers; hoops bound with ribbon and entwined with flowers; or floral balls finished with satin bows.

POSIES and
BOUQUETS

White is a great *foil* for other, more dramatic colors. Here, *classic white roses* have been combined with bold touches of *deep red* in the form of freesias and hypericum berries.

These *calla or arum lilies* are smaller and more delicate than those used for the bridal bouquet on page 46. They look very *elegant* gathered into a little sheaf with a couple of *eucharis lilies*.

This *generous* ribbon-tied bunch is designed to look as though it has just been
plucked from a country garden, with *lupines*, stocks, carnations, and sweet peas
joining roses and ripening *blackberries*.

This is another bunch inspired by the colorful informality of a cottage garden, mixing
daisies, *snowberries*, roses, stocks, delphiniums, *bupleurum*, and freesias, all tied
with *sky-blue* velvet ribbon.

When flowers are as *romantic* and beautiful as this, they deserve to be used on their own.
This bouquet of *ice-cream pink* hydrangeas and their own leaves needs nothing more than
matching satin *ribbon* to finish it.

This large bouquet has a *grand air*, although the arrangement is anything but stiff and
formal. *Bronze-green* wire-edged ribbon binds the stems of lilies, roses, kangaroo paw, and
photinia foliage and flowers.

93

This unpretentious, *cheerful* bunch of daisylike feverfew and *golden globe flowers* shows that even commonplace plants can look glorious—just use them *generously* and finish the bouquet with pretty ribbon.

This bouquet encapsulates the *spirit of spring* with a refreshing palette of white, yellow, and sappy green. *Gingham ribbon* ties a bunch of ranunculus, guelder rose, spring snowdrops, senecio, and various *narcissi*.

This small posy puts the focus on *color and form*. Galax leaves frame a tight cluster of
ranunculus, their *multipetaled heads* changing from bright orange to lime green in
the center. *Raffia* ties the stems.

Flowers for the Bridesmaids

White satin ribbon ties a small spring posy of *golden ranunculus*, some with green centers, and exquisite *white narcissi*, which will exude their wonderful *scent* in a warm atmosphere.

These delightful posies showcase *green* in all its subtle nuances, from *apple and lime* to dark, forest greens. They use ivy, Singapore orchids, guelder rose, *hellebores*, lisianthus, laurustinus, and euonymus.

Flowers for the Bridesmaids

This is not a color scheme for the faint-hearted, though the result is certainly stylish and *dramatic*. Black-red and *crimson* roses contrast with *lime-green* guelder rose, and the bouquet has been finished with burgundy ribbon.

Two *subtly different* varieties of red rose take center stage in this neat round bouquet.
They are interspersed with elegantly pointed *skimmia leaves* and their buds, while
deep red ribbon binds the stems.

Red roses with blue, rather than yellow, undertones—think of **_ruby and burgundy_**, rather than vermilion—always look particularly at home in the thin light of **_winter_**. This posy uses one variety, their stems bound with **_dark green ribbon_**.

101

This dainty posy uses flowers beloved of the Victorians, *lilies of the valley* and violets, whose delicate form and *sweet scent* guarantee their enduring appeal. Two shades of thin purple ribbon and *sequined* braid spiral around the stems.

Flowers for the Bridesmaids

By tradition, lily of the valley symbolizes sweetness and purity. Here, its *bell-like* scented
flowers have been framed by a *collar of ivy* leaves, while *white silk* ribbon with a dark
brown edge ties the stems.

Blue is *cool and calming* and, of course, closely associated with weddings. This simple but *charming* posy of grape hyacinths and *bachelor's buttons*, tied with navy ribbon, shows how attractive different tones of blue can look together.

More *sultry* than red or pink, the dramatic ***plum-purple*** tones of these ranunculus make
a very strong statement. However, a collar of snowy white *feathers* gives the arrangement
a bridal-party touch.

This floral ball is *fabulous*, frivolous, and fun. Ranunculus, pansies, cineraria, and *African violets*—all in strong pinks and purples—have been wired and inserted into an oasis ball, along with feathers and *feather butterflies*.

Flowers for the Bridesmaids

An assortment of *ribbons* ties this loose bunch of lilac and *poppy anemones*.
The unstructured shape of the bouquet and the *vibrant* colors of the flowers
give the arrangement a relaxed, informal look.

HEADDRESSES

This *floral hair comb* is easy enough to make at home. Orchids last well when cut; three pink-and-white *cymbidiums* have been used here, anchored using a hot-glue gun (available from craft suppliers) to an ordinary hair comb.

Flowers for the Bridesmaids

A wide *barette* has been used for this gorgeous *confection* of pink and white flowers.
Blooms of similar size have been chosen—delicate spray roses and *frilly carnations*—then
carefully wired onto the comb.

For a *young bridesmaid*, nothing looks more charming than a headdress of fresh flowers. Here, a mixture of *cottage-garden* favorites, among them roses, *bachelor's buttons*, and ivy, have been wired onto a headband already dotted with tiny fabric flowers.

In the hands of a skilled florist, *pansies* are not just useful bedding plants. They have many uses for wedding flowers—here, a *sumptuous* purple variety has been wired into a *bridesmaid's circlet*.

Enchanting fabric *butterflies* have been wired onto this young bridesmaid's floral hair accessory, so that they *flutter* as she moves. They accompany *pinkish-mauve* roses, green-tinged pink hydrangea flowerets, and a base of silvery gray leaves.

Flowers for the Bridesmaids

This **verdant circlet** makes the most of the fresh greens and whites of
early-summer flowering shrubs, with greenish-white **guelder rose** heads,
bridal wreath flowers and leaves, and euonymus foliage.

The *pompomlike* pink double daisies used for these headdresses can be found (along with blue and white varieties) in garden centers, sold as bedding plants. Here, however, they've been wired with ivy leaves into circlets fit for *fairies*.

Flowers for the Bridesmaids

Hydrangeas are among the few garden flowers that are *truly blue*. This variety, the color of a cloudless *summer sky*, has been wired into thick crowns and *floral balls*, embellished with pale and dark blue ribbons.

BASKETS
and other ideas

Floral balls are time-consuming to make because flowers usually need to be *wired* before being pushed into an oasis ball, but they last well and always make an *impact*. This glowing display uses tulips, roses, *snowberries*, and euonymus.

Flowers for the Bridesmaids

Another floral ball, this time in a *cooler scheme* of green, cream, and white. The *hypericum* berries, roses, and smaller *spray roses* used here have strong stems, so were all inserted straight into an oasis ball.

This floral ball is for those with a taste for the *unconventional*. While the shape is classic, the plants are not: *green* cymbidium orchids flecked with purple and skimmia leaves, all finished with sumptuous *purple* wire-edged ribbon.

122

Flowers for the Bridesmaids

These flowergirls hold small woven *baskets* filled with miniature or patio roses in warm
shades of *sugar pink*, deep pink, and golden yellow. Mint green and pale pink
ribbon *streamers* add to the fun.

Decorated hoops are a delight, harking back to nostalgic Victorian images of childhood.
This one has been covered in roses, *bridal wreath*, lisianthus, ivy, and *euonymus*, and
finished with a big white bow.

In a nod to old *customs* and rituals, these little flowergirls carry floral *"maypoles"*—in fact, broomstick handles wrapped in ribbon, topped with posies composed of pansies, double daisies, *forget-me-nots*, and columbines.

These fabulous *sequined bags* are a more *sophisticated* way for bridesmaids to carry flowers and double as presents to take home. The roses were inserted into oasis blocks and the blocks sealed with plastic wrap to keep the bags dry.

Flowers for the Bridesmaids

A basket of *pure white flowers* for an early summer wedding. *Moss* has been wired
onto the outside of the basket and ivy twisted around the handle, before filling it with
pansies and *lilies of the valley*.

Pliable *pussy willow* has been fashioned into a handle for this galvanized bucket, which overflows with the colors of *spring* in the form of grape hyacinths, *English bluebells*, and white Spanish bluebells.

Flowers for the Bridesmaids

Lilac has a *wonderful sweet scent* and, despite its name, comes in whites, *pinks*, and purples, as well as mauve. For this circlet, finished with *purple ribbons*, two varieties (along with skimmia leaves) create a pretty effect.

Baskets and Other Ideas

Boutonnieres and Corsages

Introduction

Boutonnieres are normally worn by the bridegroom, best man, groomsmen, ushers, and fathers of the couple, and consist of a single bloom or tiny posy with a sprig of foliage. Roses and carnations are classic boutonniere choices, while for gorgeous scent you could try lily of the valley, freesias, or stephanotis. Bold flowers such as calla lilies and orchids strike a modern note. Make sure that boutonnieres are securely fastened, and don't forget to give someone extra pins in case there aren't enough to go around.

Corsages may be worn by the mothers and grandmothers of the couple and are the same size or a little larger than a boutonniere. Corsages are pinned to the outfit, usually on the chest, collar, lapel, or wrist. Bear in mind that, if the wearer's clothes are made of very fine fabric, the corsage should be small and light so it doesn't drag or tear. They can also be anchored with tiny magnets, one concealed in the arrangement and the other behind the dress fabric.

A *rose* boutonniere is a classic choice, but in *searing orange* it's definitely
fun rather than fusty, its brilliantly colored petals *livening* up the dark tones
of a traditional morning suit.

Presenting boutonnieres to their wearers on a pretty tray is a small detail, but one of the many little things that can make the day *special* for all participants. Here, *deep pink roses* and ivy leaves lie on a tray with heart cut-out handles.

Instead of giving the men in the bridal party identical boutonnieres, why not use a *variety* of *complementary* flowers? From left: pink spray roses with rose leaves; *stocks* and variegated ivy; a dark red rose and ivy leaf.

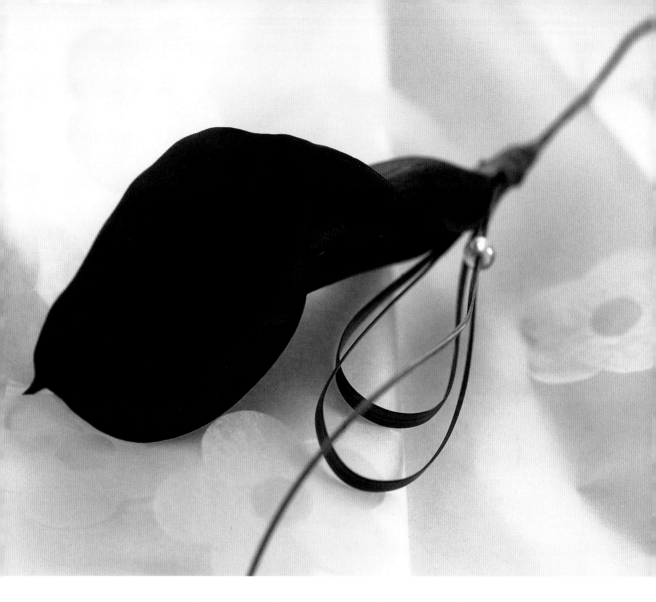

With its extraordinary sculptural shape and *intensely dark* color, this calla lily makes a striking boutonniere, accompanied by loops of bear grass, one of them threaded with a *clear glass bead* for *subtle* sparkle.

Boutonnieres, clockwise from top left: a rose with a ruffle of *cockscomb*, the stems bound in green ribbon; a white rose, gold-sprayed ***willow catkins***, and skimmia leaves; a golden rose and variegated euonymus; a rose, winter jasmine, and a bow of ***cranberry*** ribbon.

Boutonnieres and Corsages

Clockwise from top left: grape hyacinths, *galax leaves*, and narrow navy ribbon; a pink
parrot tulip and its leaf; sprigs of rosemary and copper-brown *striped ribbon*;
scented hyacinth flowerets and navy ribbon.

Boutonnieres, clockwise from top left: a rose, *hydrangea flowerets*, and ivy, their stems spiral-bound with two colors of narrow ribbon; viburnum flowers and foliage; a *moth orchid*, camellia leaves, and grosgrain ribbon; a burnt-orange gerbera with *turquoise* and lime-green ribbon.

Boutonnieres, from left: *lilac buds* with white ribbon and braid; a stem of ivy with *royal purple* ribbon; *aromatic* rosemary and dove-gray ribbon; exotic kangaroo paw and moss-green ribbon.

Gray-green narrow *velvet* ribbon tightly binds the stems of this boutonniere of white rosebuds and white *heather* (which, traditionally, is supposed to bring *good luck* to the wearer).

Cream velvet ribbon has been bound around the stems of this boutonniere—composed
of irises, *freesias*, and *mimosa*—in a distinctive crisscross pattern, showing that, even
on a small scale, there is always room for *inventiveness*.

Corsages, clockwise from top left: fragrant sweet peas, wired beads, and sequin trim;
a rose, ivy leaf, and *rosebud braid*; globe flowers, feverfew, and a galax leaf;
scented white narcissi and dark green *ruched ribbon*.

Boutonnieres and Corsages

This *classic corsage* has been wired to keep it light—particularly important if it's
to be worn on an outfit made of delicate fabric. It's composed of freesias,
hypericum berries, a rose, a large ivy leaf, and *jasmine*.

This *elegant* corsage of white spray roses, stephanotis buds, and *variegated ivy* has been injected with a bit of fun by tying the stems with *polka-dot satin* ribbon.

For an *evening reception*, give bridesmaids a *glamorous* little sequined bag full of flowers in place of a traditional corsage. Here, pansies have been chosen for their *velvety petals* and intense color.

A wrist corsage is an unusual and *stylish variation* on the corsage theme.
Here, a head of hydrangea, its petals white *tinged with green*, has been
pinned to a length of pretty floral braid.

Boutonnieres and Corsages

This *cymbidium* orchid is a practical as well as beautiful choice for a wrist corsage—orchids *last well* when cut. It's been attached with a hot-glue gun (from craft suppliers) to wide ribbon.

Flowers for the Reception

Introduction

The bride and bridesmaids' bouquets set the tone for the flowers at the reception, such as table centerpieces, chair-back decorations, favors, and decorations for the cake. However, the surroundings also help to determine the style of the reception displays. Important considerations include the level of formality or informality; whether the reception is indoors or out; whether the room's decor is traditional or modern, and so on.

Whatever style you adopt, the table arrangements mustn't detract from the main business of the day, which is eating, drinking, talking, and having fun. Towering centerpieces will impede the flow of conversation. Guests should be able to see over, under, or through arrangements easily, and remember that beautifully scented flowers will enhance their enjoyment of the celebrations.

Think creatively about the containers you use, whether you choose vases, bowls, galvanized buckets, terracotta pots, or even goldfish bowls. Oasis rings can be turned into spectacular floral wreaths to display on walls, doors, or tables. You could add candles to some of your displays, particularly if the reception is an evening one. If you want to give your guests floral favors to take home as mementoes, these could be used as part of the table decorations, perhaps doubling as placecard holders at each place setting. Flowers can transform the humblest of venues, but since they will have served their purpose by the end of the reception, encourage guests to take arrangements home with them. While you're on your honeymoon, they'll be enjoying your wedding flowers at home.

TABLE CENTERPIECES

This linear arrangement of *eucalyptus*, roses, carnations, *hypericum berries*, loosestrife, and bear grass, all in *cooling shades* of white, cream, and green, has been designed with a long rectangular table in mind.

A white and green scheme again, but this time *modern and exotic* in feel. The display features limes (brushed with petroleum jelly to prevent discoloration), chrysanthemums, *roses*, painter's palettes, and *variegated foliage*.

157

An oasis ring is the base for this *romantic arrangement*. It uses salal foliage,
hydrangeas, roses, freesias, lisianthus, and *veronicas*, with a *chunky candle* in the
center to cast a warm glow over the table.

A square glass vase houses this pretty display of roses, their *full-blown* heads interspersed with stems of *senecio* foliage. A simple centerpiece such as this relies on using *perfect blooms* in quantity to achieve its effect.

159

This centerpiece, an abundant display of roses, *crabapples*, snowberries, bupleurum, and jasmine in a *galvanized bucket*, has been designed to give a *country-garden feel* to an outdoor reception.

Another *al fresco* table setting, this time more formal and sophisticated. The fine china and crystal are complemented by a shallow *silver bowl* filled with pink spray roses, *scented stephanotis*, and variegated ivy.

161

Red, white, and green are an *ideal combination* for a winter wedding.
The carnations in this centerpiece are *richest ruby* and make a pleasing
foil for the *pure white* stephanotis and variegated ivy.

Flowers for the Reception

A *simple white pot* has been dressed up by placing it on folded satin ribbon. In it have been placed roses in an exquisite shade of *apricot*, with extra *petals* scattered down the length of the table.

This goldfish bowl makes an unexpected but *magnificent* centerpiece. A huge,
ice-cream pink peony, pink-and-white rose, and magenta Singapore orchid float
inside, and it is surrounded by more *peonies*, roses, and orchids.

A joyous display of cottage-garden favorites—lupines, stocks, carnations, sweet peas, roses, ripening *blackberries*, and Queen Anne's lace—seems to erupt from a tall *fluted glass* vase at this late-summer wedding in the country.

Many **bulbs** burst into glorious life in spring, and this centerpiece features two highly scented ones—**hyacinths** (here in indigo) and narcissi (a variety called **Paperwhite**)—in a simple, painted terracotta pot.

This delightful centerpiece also displays a **table number**, combining practicality with beauty. The painted terracotta pot, finished with a sash of ribbon, has been planted with **scented jasmine** trained over a hoop.

Elegant *slender tapers* emerge from a *cloud* of white Queen Anne's lace
and *nerines* to make a display of ethereal beauty. Since tapers don't have
a long burning time, don't light them until the meal is about the start.

This table setting has a ***grand and formal*** air, created by using fine china, crystal, and ***silverware***. An antique silver urn, filled with roses, tulips, mimosa, ***snowberries***, and senecio, is a magnificent centerpiece.

CHAIRS and
PLACE SETTINGS

An artificial wreath with *tiny blue* fabric roses has been used as a base for this circlet, hung *casually* over the back of a chair. *Fresh mimosa* has been added for a splash of cheerful yellow.

This posy of *laurel*, senecio, tulips, roses, and snowberries has been
tied to its chair with white ribbon and, with the addition of
a *handwritten tag*, also acts as a place marker.

A simple white folding chair has been gorgeously decorated for an outdoor reception. *Hosta leaves* frame *pinkish-red roses*, white-and-pink spray roses, carnations, and stephanotis buds, all tied with *green ribbon*.

Flowers for the Reception

Two *spectacular* chair decorations mark the **bride and groom's places** at the top
table. Mimosa flowers and foliage, roses, euonymus, and snowberries have been
finished with a *cascade* of variegated ivy.

This bunch of country flowers, tied with palest *apricot ribbon*, anchors one end of
a *jasmine swag* on a wide wooden bench. The arrangement includes roses, freesias,
crabapples, veronicas, and *New England asters*.

This decoration would be ideal for the *top table*, or just the bride and groom's chairs.
A combination of salal foliage, lilies, *bells of Ireland*, roses, and *jasmine*, it's firmly tied
on with twine, which is then disguised with wide ribbon.

A *twig wreath* (available from florists) can easily be dressed up with *fresh flowers*. Here,
ivy has been twined around the wreath and *shocking pink* anemones wired on before
it was secured to a chair with bright pink ribbon.

Flowers for the Reception

The base for this decoration is, again, a twig wreath, which has here been attached with *narrow ribbon* to a wall above a seating plan. Variegated ivy creates an attractive *backdrop* for pink spray roses and scented *stephanotis*.

179

This *simple treatment* for a painted wooden chair has plenty of *country charm*. A bow
of wide lilac satin ribbon hides the place where two bunches of *aromatic lavender* join,
tied end to end.

This just-opened *hydrangea head*, tied to a chair with pale blue ribbon, is beautifully *soft* in color. The idea could be recreated for next to nothing if the flowers were harvested from the *gardens* of family and friends.

Sprigs of *frothy Queen Anne's lace* and euonymus *spill out* from a dainty cone, made at home from nothing more expensive than heavy white paper. Ribbon glued to the back of the cone attaches it to the chair.

A large wreath, attached to a wall, door, or window frame, is an instant *focal point*.
Here, an oasis ring is the foundation for a display of *hydrangea heads*, small pink roses,
and *wired sequins* and butterflies.

This napkin-ring decoration consists of a *white freesia*, pink veronica, *skimmia leaf*, and skimmia buds, all wired to keep the arrangement neat and light. A sash of *moss-green velvet ribbon* finishes the look.

Colored *Moroccan tea glasses* are the perfect size for *small posies* (here, sweet peas, a rose, and greenish-white *guelder rose*) and make a decorative memento to be taken home after the wedding.

This pretty favor also acts as a *placecard holder*. A plain terracotta pot has been painted white, then potted with lily of the valley, whose *bell-like flowers* are sweetly scented, and top-dressed with moss.

This simple but stunning table setting relies on **attention to detail**. Deep, pinkish-red is a dramatic **accent color** against white, picked out by the glassware, plate rims, and **rose heads** that lie on each pristine napkin.

Napkin decorations, clockwise from top left: a *wintry sprig* of berried ivy, tied with twine; a bunch of lavender with a sash of *sheer lilac* ribbon; an aspidistra leaf, tied with *bear grass*; crabapples and narrow olive-green ribbon.

Clockwise from top left: a folded napkin, decorated with a pink *scabious*, holds a placecard; ribbon secures Queen Anne's lace and euonymus; *napkin holders* of wide, gray ribbon, with guests' names attached, secure rosemary sprigs; a pink lisianthus is tucked under *oyster-colored* ribbon.

FLOWERS
for the CAKE

Sophisticated and *modern*, this cake's three tiers have been simply decorated with *opalescent* icing "pearls." A cluster of flawless white *eucharis lilies* on the top tier is the only extra embellishment.

Square tiers, iced in a basketweave pattern, take the place of round ones to make this glorious cake. The three tiers overflow with *full-blown roses* in subtle shades of *palest pink*, apricot, cream, and white.

Hypericum berries and *pink bouvardia* have been made into posies, then anchored to each tier of this cake by pushing a pin through their bound stems. More bouvardia, cut very short, forms the domed *cake topper*.

This highly romantic and very *elegant* cake consists of four stacked tiers, decorated with graduated icing "pearls." Posies of ice-cream pink hydrangeas, stephanotis, and *snowberries* complete the pretty picture.

A thoroughly *feminine* cake for a late-summer wedding: the tiers have been covered
in *blush-pink icing* and a simple piped design, then finished with individual
flowerets from a pink hydrangea.

Green and white is always a calming and *refreshing* combination. Here, tiny sprigs
of ***bupleurum***, whose frothy flower heads are ***lime green***, lend their
discreet charm to a simple cake.

The tiers of this cake have been simply iced with a tiny *all-over pattern*, then dressed with luscious, pinkish-red roses, *white-and-pink* spray roses, aromatic lavender, and *glossy galax* leaves.

Gleaming ruffles decorate this elaborate, *indulgent* chocolate cake. Large *poppy anemones* in vivid shades of red, pink, and purple, partnered by *sage leaves*, stand out boldly against the dark background.

FLOWERS
as FAVORS

This miniature galvanized bucket holds a *modest but charming* display of Queen Anne's lace and *euonymus*. White *tissue paper* lines the container, kept dry by a waterproofing inner layer of plastic.

A cluster of white *spray roses*, some fully open and some *still in bud* so
they will continue to give a display once a guest takes the favor home, sits
in an elegant *silver pot*.

This galvanized bucket, complete with diminutive *gardener's fork*, has been planted
with *grape hyacinths*, whose dainty, *intensely blue* flowers appear in the spring.
It does double duty as a placecard holder.

Small *terracotta* pots are inexpensive and easy to turn into decorative favors. This one has been sprayed silver and filled with an unusual combination of sea holly, whose *steel-blue cones* are surrounded by *silvery* bracts, and senecio.

205

This wicker basket, its handle decorated with a bow of **cobalt-blue** ribbon, has been filled with stem upon stem of *fragrant bluebells*, ready to be tied into posies for wedding guests.

With its *glorious scent* and delightful flowers, lavender's a *star plant*. Here, small bunches of dried lavender, the stems stripped of their gray-green leaves, have been tied with sheer white ribbon to be *handed out* to guests.

Flowers as Favors

Planning

Flower checklist

Bride's bouquet

Bouquets or posies for the bridesmaids

Corsages for the mothers

Boutonnieres for the groom, best man,
groomsmen, ushers, and fathers

Arrangements for the church or civil venue

Arrangements for the reception

Suggested color themes

Single-color schemes—all white, for
instance—are one possibility. However,
they can look monotonous, so blend
deeper and paler shades of one color for
variety, and remember the value of foliage.

Combining colors is the other option.
A color wheel is a visual way of dividing
the spectrum and a useful tool since it
shows which colors create contrasting
partnerships and which are harmonious.
Opposite or contrasting pairs include red
(or pink) and green; blue and yellow;
purple and orange. Harmonious pairings
include pink and purple; blue and green;
yellow and orange. In general, dark or
very bright colors need the most skillful
handling; pastels are easier to use.

White is associated with purity and serenity.
Ivory and cream are often more flattering
than pure white, and white flowers usually
have undertones—yellow, pink, blue, or
green—that warm or cool them. White is
an ideal foil for other colors and can be
combined with any of them.

Yellows can be cool or warm, and the two types don't mix well. Greenish yellows blend well with green, cream, white, or soft blue; golden yellows are a good match for oranges and warm reds.

Orange can be a challenge. As apricot, peach, and buff, it's easier to use, mixed with cream or buttery yellow. Intense orange combines well with warm yellow, gold, terracotta, or warm reds; or it can be cooled with blue, green, or purple.

Red is the most powerful primary color. The addition of green, white, or cream helps to tone it down. Blue reds can be mixed with reddish purples; even pink can be used with red, but only with great care.

Pink is feminine and romantic. Avoid mixing cool pinks with blue undertones and warm pinks with yellow undertones. Pink and green is a classic combination; cool pinks look beautiful with purple, blue, and silver; coral can be combined with oranges and pinkish reds for tropical sizzle.

Purple ranges from lilac and mauve to plum and almost black. Deep purples work with dark reds, blues, or pinks for a jewellike effect. Paler shades look good with soft blues and pale pinks. Dark purples with red undertones can be partnered with orange.

Blue ranges from true blues to purplish shades such as lavender. It blends well with white, cream, cool pink, and purple; true blue works well with yellow.

Green is an invaluable partner for other colors, and foliage plays a key part in most floral displays. Lime or apple greens look good with white, cream, blue, and yellow; contrasting green with red, pink, or purple can also be very effective.

Flower buying and care tips

- A commercial flower food will prolong the life of cut flowers. Sugar, sparkling lemon-lime sodas, or aspirin added to the water will also keep flowers healthier longer.

- If you're using flowers from your own garden, they may not last as long as commercially grown flowers. Garden flowers, like bought flowers, should stand in fresh water before use.

- Make sure that any containers used for soaking flowers are clean and bacteria-free. Rinse them with water containing a little bleach before using.

- Look for bright yellow stamens on lilies; old lilies (of all varieties) have dark stamens.

- Make sure lily stamens are removed; their pollen stains anything it touches bright orange.

- Spray table arrangements with water to keep them fresh and the oasis moist.

- Keep all finished arrangements somewhere cool and dark, but don't be tempted to store any flowers, including boutonnieres and corsages, in the fridge.

- The length of a teardrop bouquet should be tailored to the height of the bride: the taller the bride, the longer the bouquet can be. For a petite bride, a tied bunch is probably more flattering.

- For pinning boutonnieres to lapels, buy pearl-headed pins, which look more special than normal straight pins.

- Some of the longest-lasting flowers are chrysanthemums, carnations, orchids, roses, tulips, and calla lilies. Sweet peas and poppy anemones, though beautiful, have a short life once cut.

- Prices of exotic flowers such as callas and orchids can rise markedly during the peak wedding months (May to July), or if supplies are low. If you're on a budget, go for flowers less prone to fluctuations in price, such as roses and carnations.

Working with a florist

When you're looking for a florist, begin by asking friends for recommendations. Your caterer or reception venue may also have some ideas. Otherwise, make appointments with several local florists. Ask if they have a portfolio, so you can see whether you like their work. Look for someone who is helpful, sympathetic to your requests, has plenty of ideas, and is easy to get on with.

If possible, take along fabric swatches or pictures of your dress and your attendants' outfits, since they're the natural starting point for choosing a color scheme. If you've been inspired by books or magazines, take these along, particularly if you don't know the names of the flowers you like. Look at flowers in the shop and don't be afraid to ask what they are if you're not sure.

Tell your florist what your budget is. Remember that the more complicated and time-consuming the arrangement (such as wired bouquets, floral "trees," garlands, or floral arches), the more expensive it is. Discuss what props you might want (vases, candelabra, pedestals) and ask who will do the arranging on the day. If the florist is unfamiliar with the venues you're using, ask if they will visit them to help you both decide what sort of arrangements you need. Failing that, show them photographs.

Once you've decided what you want, get a written estimate. Find out when the flowers will be delivered and give someone the task of being there to receive them. Ask for bouquets to be labeled, so there isn't any confusion about which is which.

Flowers for all seasons

Nowadays, many flowers are imported and available all year round. Examples include alstroemeria, carnations, chrysanthemums, freesias, gerberas, gypsophila, lilies, orchids, and roses. If you'd like to incorporate a seasonal element into your floral displays, try some of the following.

Spring Anemones, bluebells, camellias, crocuses, forget-me-nots, grape hyacinths, hyacinths, lilies of the valley, narcissi, pansies, ranunculus, tulips, violets.

Summer Bachelor's buttons, campanulas, daisies, delphiniums, hydrangeas, gypsophila, jasmine, lady's mantle, larkspurs, peonies, phlox, roses, scabious, stocks, sweet peas.

Fall Amaranthus, chrysanthemums, cosmos, dahlias, hydrangeas, Japanese anemones, New England asters, scabious.

Winter Heather, hellebores, irises, primulas, snowdrops, winter jasmine.

Flower directory

Agapanthus (*Agapanthus*)
Summer flowers with tall stems and
large heads of blue or white bell-shaped
blooms. Good for adding height to
arrangements.

Allium (*Allium*)
Globe-headed purple flowers that can
make a wonderful impact in big displays.
Good for adding blue tones to an
arrangement. Alliums can smell of
onions as they age.

Asparagus fern (*Asparagus densiflorus*)
An exceptionally delicate and feathery fern,
suitable for romantic arrangements and
softening the outline of a bouquet.

Aspidistra (*Aspidistra*)
Large, smooth, glossy dark green leaves that
can make a bouquet "collar."

Bachelor's button (*Centaurea cyanus*)
A true blue flower—relatively rare in the
flower world. Synonymous with summer in
the countryside.

Bells of Ireland (*Molucella*)
Tall stems of unusual green flowers, which
can exude a minty aroma.

Bluebell or Bluebonnet
(*Hyacinthoides non-scripta*)
Traditional spring favorite.

Bouvardia (*Bouvardia*)
An excellent bridal flower available in pink,
mauve, and white.

Calla or arum lily (*Zantedeschia aethiopica*)
Dramatic, sculptural blooms; expensive in
the summer months.

Camellia (*Camellia*)
Flowers are white, pink, or red, while the

leaves are dark, glossy, and very attractive. Camellia flowers are useful for winter weddings as an alternative to roses, while the hardy leaves are perfect for wiring and using in boutonnieres.

Carnation (*Dianthus*)
Long lasting, excellent value, and available in a huge color range. Popular for boutonnieres. Also known as pinks.

Chrysanthemum (*Chrysanthemum*)
Exceptionally long lasting and very good value for money. Available in a variety of colors and forms, including the spidery shamrock chrysanthemum.

Daffodil (*Narcissus*)
Quintessential spring flowers in colors from white to deep yellow. Many of the miniature varieties are scented.

Daisy (*Argyranthemum frutescens*)
Cheerful white flowers, ideal for summer posies.

Eucalyptus (*Eucalyptus*)
Attractive foliage with small, aromatic, gray-green globular leaves.

Eucharis lily (*Eucharis*)
Exceptionally elegant white flowers.

Euonymus (*Euonymus*)
Attractive foliage found in many backyards. The leaves can be variegated with white or gold, and some varieties produce pink or red fall color.

Forget-me-not (*Myosotis*)
Unpretentious, very pretty blue and pink flowers found in many yards. Flowers prolifically all spring.

Freesia (*Freesia*)
Good value scented flowers on arching stems, which can provide extra shape to an arrangement. They come in many colors.

Galax (*Galax*)
Large, glossy green leaves.

Ginger lily (*Alpinia*)
Colorful tropical flowers. Expensive but striking and dramatic, they would be ideal for a non-traditional ceremony.

Glory lily (*Gloriosa superba*)
Exotic red blooms edged with gold.

Grape hyacinth (*Muscari*)
Synonymous with spring, in colors from pale to deep blue. Useful for reception table pots and decorations.

Guelder rose (*Viburnum opulus*)
Pompomlike white blooms from a popular shrub.

Heliconia (*Heliconia*)
Sculptural tropical blooms in spicy colors.

Hellebore (*Helleborus*)
Winter flowering and so useful for winter weddings. Subtly beautiful flowers in green, pink to deep purple, and white.

Hosta (*Hosta*)
Large glossy leaves, often variegated and available in many shades of green. Useful for table arrangements.

Hyacinth (*Hyacinthus*)
Highly scented, they are useful for table decorations and come in a good color range from white to yellow, blue, pink, and purple.

Hydrangea (*Hydrangea*)
Useful for late summer and early fall color, the huge flower heads come in white, pink, blue, mauve, lime green, and even red.

Hypericum (*Hypericum*)
Green, orange, and cream berried foliage. Very useful for filling gaps in arrangements. Also known as St. John's Wort.

Iceland poppy (*Papaver croceum*)
Available in white, yellow, and burnt orange. Before using, condition the cut stems by singeing with a match.

Iris (*Iris*)
Both winter and summer flowering varieties are available, in a huge color range, often white, yellow, blue, and purple.

Ivy (*Hedera helix*)
Ivy is found in many gardens, but can also be purchased. Comes in many variegated forms as well as plain green.

Jasmine (*Jasminum*)
There are winter and summer jasmines.

Lady's mantle (*Alchemilla mollis*)
The frothy lime-green flowers are a very useful foil for other flower colors.

Lavender (*Lavandula*)
Useful for adding scent to a bouquet or table arrangement.

Lily (*Lilium*)
Spectacular large flowers that make a real impact in a bouquet, in many colors. Many varieties are highly scented.

Lily of the valley (*Convallaria majalis*)
A traditional wedding favorite, beautifully scented. The small, delicate flowers are best suited to a small posy or a table arrangement.

Lisianthus (*Eustoma*)
The flowers, often in white, lilac, or pink, are reminiscent of roses. Good value.

Loosestrife (*Lysimachia*)
Some types sparse in summer. Long, elegant tapered flowers, useful as vertical accents.

Lupine (*Lupinus*)
Cottage-garden favorites. Tall and dramatic, they are available in a wide color range.

New England aster (*Aster novi-belgii*)
Useful for late summer and fall color, usually in whites, pinks, and purples.

Orchid
This large family of flowers includes the varieties **Singapore orchids** (*Dendrobium*), **cymbidium**, and **moth orchids** (*Phalaenopsis*). They are expensive, but make excellent wedding flowers; they are available in a wide choice of shades, extremely long-lasting, and exquisite. Even if used sparingly, they will still make an impact.

Painter's palette (*Anthurium*)
Impressive sculptural blooms that bruise very easily.

Peony (*Paeonia*)
Often the first true flowers of summer. Huge, blowsy flowers in colors ranging from white to deep pink, sometimes scented. The pale pink Sarah Bernhardt variety lasts well.

Poppy anemone (*Anemone coronaria De Caen*)
Large, open flowers with bold black centers, in blue, pink, red, and white.

Queen Anne's lace (*Anthriscus sylvestris*)
Delicate white flowers found in the countryside, but also grown commercially.

Ranunculus (*Ranunculus*)
Beautiful, tightly furled flowers in an unusual color range.

Rose (*Rosa*)
A very good all-round flower for all kinds of wedding arrangements, available in myriad colors. There are small-flowered spray roses as well as large varieties. Bear in mind that commercially grown roses are usually scentless.

Scabious (*Scabiosa*)
Pretty summer and early autumn flowers in pastel shades.

Skimmia (*Skimmia*)
A useful foliage shrub for all sorts of arrangements, with dark green leaves and white flowers. If you want the red berries, they are available in winter only. The leaves are good used in boutonnieres with smaller rose varieties.

Snapdragon (*Antirrhinum*)
Cottage-garden favorite in a wide range of pretty, bright colors.

Stephanotis (*Stephanotis floribunda*)
Exquisite, scented, white waxy flowers that begin as decorative buds.

Stock (*Matthiola*)
Traditional country-garden flowers, in pretty pastels including white, pink, and lilac. They are usually scented and are good value.

Sweet pea (*Lathyrus odoratus*)
Not very long lasting, but beautiful flowers in a huge range of colors including white, purple, pink, and sometimes red. Well known for their perfume, but commercially grown varieties are not always scented.

Tulip (*Tulipa*)
Long-lasting, good-value flowers in a huge range of colors and forms, including ruffled and striped varieties.

Veronica (*Veronica*)
Elegant, tapering spires of flowers, usually in white, purple, or pink. Useful as a contrasting form to round flowers.

Flower matching chart

SCHEME: **Fresh white and green**

BRIDE

p17 Bouquet of peonies, roses, dill, and bridal wreath

BRIDAL PARTY

p115 Bridesmaid's circlet of guelder rose, bridal wreath, and euonymus

p124 Bridesmaid's hoop of roses, bridal wreath, lisianthus, ivy, and euonymus

• Try rose or lisianthus boutonnieres with ivy or euonymus for foliage

RECEPTION

p168 Table centerpiece of Queen Anne's lace and nerines or try arrangements of peonies, roses, guelder rose, bridal wreath, ivy, and euonymus

p182 Chair back of Queen Anne's lace and euonymus

p189 Top right, napkin decoration of Queen Anne's lace and euonymus

p197 Cake with bupleurum

p202 Favor of Queen Anne's lace with euonymus

SCHEME: **Classic white**

BRIDE

p18 Bouquet of roses, loosestrife, lilac, and eucalyptus

BRIDAL PARTY

p121 Bridesmaid's ball of roses and hypericum berries

p145 Corsage of rose, hypericum berries, freesias, ivy, and jasmine

• Try boutonnieres of white spray roses and green hypericum berries

RECEPTION

p156 Table centerpiece of roses, carnations, hypericum berries, loosestrife, bear grass, and eucalyptus

p167 Table centerpiece of white jasmine

p203 Favor of white spray roses

• Try chair decorations of white or cream roses, lime-green carnations, and eucalyptus

SCHEME: Romantic pink

BRIDE

p23   Bouquet of roses, stocks, and freesias

BRIDAL PARTY

p111   Hair accessory of spray roses and carnations

p126   Bridesmaid's bags filled with roses

•   Try bridesmaids' posies of white, cream, and pink roses and carnations, and boutonnieres of smaller spray roses in the same colors

RECEPTION

p158   Table centerpiece of hydrangeas, roses, freesias, lisianthus, veronica, and salal

p183   Wreath of roses and hydrangeas

p195   Cake decoration of hydrangea, stephanotis, and snowberries

•   Try chair decorations of pink roses and lisianthus, and white freesias

SCHEME: Summer in the garden

BRIDE

•   Try a larger version of the bridesmaid's bouquet, with lupines, roses, stocks, carnations, sweet peas, and blackberries

BRIDAL PARTY

p90   Bridesmaid's bouquet of lupines, roses, stocks, carnations, sweet peas, and blackberries

p111   Hair accessory of spray roses and carnations

p135   Rose boutonnieres

RECEPTION

p165   Table centerpiece of lupines, roses, stocks, sweet peas, blackberries, carnations, and Queen Anne's lace

p174   Chair back of roses, carnations, stephanotis, and hosta leaves

p198   Cake decoration of roses, lavender, and galax leaves

•   Try favors of pale and deep pink spray roses in floral tea or coffee cups

SCHEME: True blue

BRIDE

p30 Bouquet of hydrangeas, delphiniums, sea holly, and ivy

BRIDAL PARTY

p117 Bridesmaids' hydrangea circlets and balls

• Try hydrangea posies for the bridesmaids, and boutonnieres of wired hydrangea flowerets or bachelor's buttons

RECEPTION

• Try table centerpieces of delphiniums, hydrangeas, and sea holly, with hydrangea flowerets on the cake similar to p195

p181 Hydrangea chair decoration

• Try napkin decorations of delphinium and hydrangea flowerets

SCHEME: Sweet lilac

BRIDE

p31 Bouquet of white and mauve lilac

p43 Bouquet of lilac and poppy anemones

BRIDAL PARTY

p107 Bridesmaid's bouquet of lilac and poppy anemones

p129 Bridesmaid's circlet of lilac and skimmia

• Try poppy anemone boutonnieres

RECEPTION

• Try centerpieces of white and mauve lilac and a cake decoration of poppy anemones

• Try decorating chair backs with lilac heads tied on with purple ribbon, similar to p180 or p181

SCHEME: Winter reds

BRIDE

p38 Bouquet of roses, senecio, and galax

p60 Bouquet of roses and aspidistra

p62 Bouquet of roses, amaryllis, and jasmine

BRIDAL PARTY

p100 Bridesmaid's bouquet of roses and skimmia

p101 Bridesmaid's bouquet of roses

• Try red rose boutonnieres

RECEPTION

• Try table centerpieces with red roses and amaryllis, and dark evergreen foliage, with candles if the reception goes on after dark. Decorate the cake with red roses and jasmine

SCHEME: Modern white

BRIDE		BRIDAL PARTY		RECEPTION	
p24	Bouquet of calla lilies	p89	Bridesmaid's posy of calla lilies and eucharis lilies	p157	Table centerpiece of painter's palettes, limes, carnations, and roses
p46	Bouquet of calla lilies and bear grass	•	Try white calla lily boutonnieres similar to p137	•	Try placing long-stemmed calla lilies in tall glass vases

SCHEME: Elegant simplicity

BRIDE		BRIDAL PARTY		RECEPTION	
p51	Bouquet of eucharis lilies	p89	Bridesmaid's posy of calla lilies and eucharis lilies	•	Try clear glass vases filled with long-stemmed eucharis lilies
p74	Wrist corsage of eucharis lilies			p192	Cake decoration of eucharis lilies
•	Try pinning single eucharis lilies in the bride's hair				

SCHEME: Golden wedding

BRIDE		BRIDAL PARTY		RECEPTION	
p52	Bouquet of tulips	p120	Bridesmaid's ball of tulips, roses, and snowberries	p169	Table centerpiece of roses, tulips, snowberries, mimosa, and senecio
		p138	Bottom right, rose boutonniere	p173	Chair back of laurel, senecio, roses, tulips, and snowberries
				p175	Chair back of roses, mimosa, snowberries, ivy, and euonymus
				•	Try golden spray roses on the cake

Ribbons and accessories

Flowers are the stars of any bouquet, but just as the right accessories can make an outfit, finishing an arrangement with gorgeous trimmings heightens its beauty.

Ribbon is incredibly useful for this because it comes in so many different finishes, fabrics, patterns, and colors. Even the simplest bunched posy can be given a bridal look by finishing it with a pretty bow. Go and browse around a good notions department to see the different types on offer: satin and taffeta (which can be plain or patterned, with a plain or decorative edge); sheer (these can sometimes be "shot" for extra shimmer); grosgrain (which has a distinctive ribbed texture); jacquard (with a woven, rather than printed, pattern); velvet; wire-edged; metallic; pleated; and ruched.

Ribbon can be used to bind the stems of a bouquet or posy completely (see page 41), which looks decorative and serves the useful practical purpose of making it more comfortable to hold for a long time. Alternatively, ribbon can be used just to tie the stems under the head of the bouquet (see page 42), finishing in a bow. A good florist should be able to arrange ribbon into various sorts of bows, some with multiple loops for an extravagant look (see page 54). Wide wire-edged ribbons are particularly useful for

bouquets because they keep their shape so well when fashioned into a bow.

There's no reason to limit yourself to one type of ribbon, of course, and very pretty effects can be created by layering sheer and satin ribbon; or combining wide and narrow ribbons; or ribbons in different shades (see page 29). Sheer fabrics such as organdy and net can also be used to create a "collar" around a bouquet (see pages 37 and 50), and fine tulle can envelop a bouquet for an ultra-romantic, soft-focus look (see page 49). Leaving ribbon ends long can create a more dramatic look (see page 24), and adding ribbon streamers to a bouquet (see page 32) gives it a more traditional, rustic look. Narrow ribbon, braid, and other trims are useful for finishing boutonnieres and corsages, and although these arrangements are small in scale, there is plenty of scope for creativity in the way the stems are decorated (see pages 140 to 141).

The usual way to secure ribbon to the stem of a bouquet is with pearl-headed pins, which can themselves be further decorated by threading beads onto them (see page 26). Beads, wired beads, or sequins can be used for glamorous sparkle, perhaps threaded onto fine grasses (see page 46), or tucked in among flowers (see page 23). Artificial butterflies can be wired and used alongside flowers (see pages 106 and 183), as can feathers (see page 105). In a much more contemporary vein, sculptural effects can be created by using wire to bind stems and encircle bouquets (see pages 58 and 70). Very fine wire can be worked into a lattice to give a lighter effect not unlike spun sugar (see page 71).

Paint may sound like an unlikely ingredient in floristry, but sprays have their uses. In winter, bare branches, twigs, and dried seed heads can be transformed with metallic spray paint. Flowers, too, can be sprayed, but for the best effect, this needs to be done very lightly, so the petals are merely touched with color. Another unusual technique is to mist flowers with spray adhesive (from art suppliers), then apply glitter. All these effects work best on flowers that have a good shape and petals that aren't too flimsy, such as roses.

The language of flowers

It is believed that the idea of associating meanings or
sentiments with particular flowers was introduced to Europe
from Asia in the eighteenth century. However, it was the
Victorians who popularized the idea in the English-speaking
world, allowing through flowers the expression of emotions
that couldn't be voiced openly in polite society. It may add to
your enjoyment of the flowers you choose for your wedding
to know that they have a special meaning.

Alstroemeria . . . . *Friendship*
Amaryllis . . . . *Splendid beauty*
Bachelor's button . . . . *Delicacy*
Calla lily . . . . *Delicacy*
Camellia . . . . *Perfect beauty*
Carnation . . . . *Pure and deep love; woman's love*
Cherry blossom . . . . *Spiritual beauty*
Chrysanthemum . . . . *Truth*

Chrysanthemum, red . . . .*In love*

Crocus . . . .*Youthful gladness; cheerfulness*

Daffodil . . . .*Regard*

Dahlia . . . .*Forever thine*

Daisy . . . .*Innocence*

Daisy, double . . . .*Enjoyment*

Freesia . . . .*Innocence*

Gardenia . . . .*Ecstasy*

Guelder rose . . . .*Age*

Gypsophila . . . .*Fruitful marriage*

Heather, white . . . .*Good luck*

Honeysuckle . . . .*Fidelity; the band of love*

Hyacinth . . . .*Constancy*

Hyacinth, white . . . .*Unobtrusive loveliness*

Iris . . . .*A message*

Ivy . . . .*Matrimony*

Lavender . . . .*Love and devotion*

Lilac, purple . . . .*First emotions of love*

Lilac, white . . . .*Youth*

Lily . . . .*Purity; modesty*

Lily of the valley . . . . *Return of happiness*

Mallow . . . . *Sweetness; good and kind*

Marjoram . . . . *Blushes*

Mimosa . . . . *Modesty; delicate feelings*

Orchid . . . . *A belle*

Palm . . . . *Victory*

Pansy . . . . *You occupy my thoughts*

Pansy, yellow . . . . *Think of me*

Peony . . . . *Happy marriage*

Periwinkle . . . . *Sweet memories*

Phlox . . . . *United hearts*

Polyanthus . . . . *Confidence*

Primrose . . . . *Eternal youth*

Ranunculus . . . . *Radiant with charms*

Rose . . . . *Love; beauty*

Rose, blush . . . . *If you love me, you will find it out*

Rose, cabbage . . . . *Ambassador of love*

Rose, full blown . . . . *You are beautiful*

Rose, full white . . . . *I am worthy of you*

Rose, red . . . . *I love you*

Rosebud . . . . *Youth*

Snowdrop . . . . *A friend in adversity*

Stock . . . . *Lasting beauty*

Sunflower . . . . *Adoration*

Sweet pea . . . . *Departure*

Tulip . . . . *Fame*

Veronica . . . . *Fidelity*

Violet . . . . *Modesty*

Source list

Associations

American Institute of Floral Designers
410-752-3318
www.aifd.org
Offers directory of more than 1,200 certified floral designers nationwide.

International Flower Picture Database
www.flowerweb.com
In-depth resource for floral designers, novice and otherwise.

Society of American Florists
800-336-4743
www.aboutflowers.com
Consumer information from the floral trade's national association.

Craft supplies
From glue guns to gift bags.

Crate and Barrel
650 Madison Avenue
New York, NY 10022
212-308-0011
www.crateandbarrel.com
Vases and containers.

Hobby Lobby
405-745-1100
www.hobbylobby.com

JoAnn Fabrics & Crafts
800-525-4951
www.joann.com

Michael's
800-Michaels
www.michaels.com

Renaissance Ribbons
P.O. Box 699
Oregon House, CA 95962
530-692-0842
www.renaissanceribbons.com

WireStore
888-773-8769
www.wirestore.com
Wide selection of wire frames for bouquets and other arrangements.

Floral Designers

Big Rose
877-701-7673
www.bigrose.com
Specializes in bridal kits.

Bridal Blooms & Creations
972-907-8804
www.bridal blooms.com
Sophisticated floral design.

The Knot
www.theknot.com/flowers
Search this bridal site for a local florist, plus plenty of information and inspiration for your wedding.

ProFlowers
800-776-3569
www.proflowers.com
Wide selection of bouquets available online, including roses awarded "best value" by the *Wall Street Journal*.

Phillip's 1-800-FLORALS
800-356-7257
www.800florals.com
Purveyor of quality bouquets since 1923.

Romantic Flowers
206-250-8228
www.romanticflowers.com
Wedding flowers are the specialty of this romantic site.

Index

Picture Credits

Photography by Craig Fordham, arrangements and styling by Jane Durbridge:
Endpapers, pages 6, 7, 10, 14–15, 17, 19, 21, 24, 28, 30, 31, 32, 33, 36, 37, 38, 39, 40, 41, 42, 43, 44–45, 47, 49, 50, 53, 54, 55, 56–57, 58, 59, 61, 62, 63, 64, 66, 67, 68, 69, 70, 71, 72–73, 75, 76, 77, 78, 79, 82, 84, 85, 86–87, 93, 94, 95, 96, 98, 99, 100, 102, 103, 104, 106, 107, 108–109, 113, 115, 116, 117, 118–119, 122, 123, 124, 125, 127, 128, 129, 138–139 all, 144 all, 147, 206, 208, 211 all, 213, 215 all, 218l, 219c, 219r, 221r

Photography by Polly Wreford, styling by Margaret Caselton:
Pages 2–3, 4–5, 8, 9, 16, 29, 34–35, 48, 51, 52, 74, 81, 89, 90, 91, 92, 101, 111, 112, 120, 132–133, 135, 136, 142, 143, 148, 150, 152–153, 154–155, 159, 160, 161, 162, 165, 167, 169, 170–171, 172, 173, 174, 175, 176, 178, 179, 186, 187, 188bl, 190–191, 192, 193, 195, 198, 199, 203, 204, 218r, 231a

Photography by Polly Wreford, styling by Mary Norden:
Pages 1, 12, 13, 25, 65, 97, 140ar, 141, 150, 163, 166, 168, 180, 181, 182, 188ar, 188br, 189 all, 196, 197, 200–201, 202, 205, 219l

Photography by Carolyn Barber, arrangements by Nancy Ursell, styling by Liz Belton:
Pages 18, 20, 22, 23, 46, 60, 105, 110, 121, 126, 130, 134, 137, 145, 149, 156, 157, 158, 177, 184, 194, 217 all, 231c, 231b

Photography by Carolyn Barber, arrangements by Sania Pell:
Pages 26, 183

Other Photography

Sandra Lane
Pages 140al, 140bl, 140br, 146, 188al, 229

Pia Tryde
Pages 220c, 220r, 221l, 221c, 235

Caroline Arber
Pages 27, 80, 114, 207

Melanie Eclare
Pages 222c, 223c, 223r

Francesca Yorke
Pages 222l, 223l, 233c

Henry Bourne
Pages 220l, 233b

David Brittain
Page 185

Peter Cassidy
Page 222r

James Merrell
Page 218c

David Montgomery
Page 233a

Polly Wreford
Page 164

Viv Yeo
Page 88